Don't You Dare Give Up

Don't You Dare Give Up

Tony Medley

MEDLEY

CONTENTS

Publisher: *Medley Publisher Group*

First Printing, 2025

ISBN (Paperback): 979-8-9934305-9-1
ISBN (eBook): 979-8-9940033-0-5

This book is a work of nonfiction based on biblical teaching, pastoral experience, and counseling principles. It is provided for spiritual and educational purposes only and is not intended to replace licensed mental health care, legal counsel, or medical treatment. Readers should seek appropriate professional guidance when needed.

Unless otherwise noted, Scripture quotations are from the King James Version (KJV).

Printed in the United States of America

Introduction

When Life Presses Hard

If you are reading this book, chances are you know what it feels like to be tired, tested, and maybe even on the edge of giving up. Life can press against us in ways we never expected—losses that cut deep, disappointments that shake our confidence, delays that make us question whether God has forgotten us.

You are not alone. Every believer, from the prophets of old to the apostles of the New Testament, faced seasons of adversity and affliction. What makes their stories so powerful is not that they avoided trials, but that they held on to God through them.

God's Invitation

In Jeremiah 33:3, God makes a promise that still echoes today:

"Call unto me, and I will answer thee, and show thee great and mighty things, which thou knowest not."

This verse is not just poetry—it is a covenant invitation. God is saying, "Don't give up. Call on Me, and I will meet you in your struggle with revelation, with strength, with victory you never imagined."

Your calling, your purpose, and your destiny are too important to be abandoned. The enemy wants you to loosen your grip, but God is saying, "Hold on to Me. Don't you dare give up."

Why This Book

I wrote this book as a counselor, a pastor, and a fellow traveler. I have listened to tears in counseling sessions, prayed through sleepless nights with those who were hurting, and walked through my own valleys. I know what it feels like to wonder if tomorrow will ever be different.

But I also know the faithfulness of God. I have seen Him lift broken hearts, restore marriages, heal the sick, and open doors no one could shut. I have witnessed Him turn pain into purpose and tears into testimonies.

This book is not just about what you're going through—it's about the God who goes through it with you.

What to Expect

This journey is laid out in 27 chapters, grouped into seven parts. Each part will walk you through stages of the believer's life:

- Strength for the Journey – Understanding your heart and mind in Christ.
- Standing Bold in Christ – Learning to live with confidence and assurance.
- Drawing Near to God – Cultivating intimacy, truth, and faith.
- Endurance Through Trials – Facing adversity and trusting in deliverance.
- Living in Victory – Believing, trusting, and walking in triumph.
- Pressing Toward the Prize – Choosing persistence when quitting looks easier.
- More Than a Conqueror – Living the lifestyle of decisive victory.

Each chapter will not only unpack biblical truth but also provide counseling insights, practical steps, and reflection questions—tools you can use in your daily walk.

My Heart for You

This book is not about lofty ideas or unreachable standards. It is about real faith for real struggles. It is for the weary parent, the grieving spouse, the discouraged dreamer, and the believer who feels like they've prayed all they can pray.

If you've ever whispered, "I can't do this anymore," this book is my response to you:

Don't you dare give up.

God has not forgotten you. His promises still stand. And He has placed within you the heart, the mind, the faith, and the authority to overcome.

So turn the page. Let us walk together through these truths. By the time you reach the end of this book, my prayer is that you will not only believe in victory but live as one who has already conquered—because in Christ, you have.

Preface

Every believer, no matter how strong their faith may appear, comes face to face with moments of weakness, fear, and uncertainty. I know this not just from years of pastoring and counseling others, but from walking through valleys of my own. There were times I wanted to stop, to step back, to let go. Times when the weight of life felt too heavy to carry another step.

But in those moments, God met me. His Word became my lifeline. His Spirit became my strength. His promises became the anchor that kept me from drifting away. And over the years, I have learned this truth: the greatest victories are often born out of the fiercest battles.

This book, Don't You Dare Give Up, was birthed out of prayer, tears, and a relentless pursuit of the God who promised never to leave us nor forsake us. It is not just a collection of sermons or teachings—it is a counselor's heart poured onto pages, meant to walk beside you in your midnight hour.

You will find in these chapters a journey. We begin by understanding the heart, mind, and spirit. We move into the call to boldness, truth, and faith. We face the reality of adversity and affliction, only to discover God's unshakable promise of deliverance. And then, as the journey reaches its height, we step into victory, learn to believe and keep believing, exercise the authority of the Kingdom, and live as overcomers.

My prayer for you is simple: that as you read, hope will rise. That as you reflect, your faith will deepen. That when you feel the weight of giving up pressing on your chest, you will hear the Spirit whisper, "Don't you dare give up—I am with you."

This book is not meant to sit on your shelf. It is a companion, a counselor, a reminder that the God who called you is faithful. He will finish what He started. And when the storm passes, you will not just survive—you will stand as more than a conqueror.

With love and faith,

DR. TONY E. MEDLEY SR.

Foreword

Life is a journey filled with valleys and mountaintops, storms and sunshine, victories and battles. Along the way, we encounter moments that test the very fabric of our faith. These are the seasons when doubt whispers, fear looms large, and giving up seems easier than pressing on. Yet, it is precisely in those moments that God calls us to stand, to believe, and to hold fast to His promises.

Don't You Dare Give Up is more than a book—it is a divine reminder that God has equipped you with everything you need not just to survive, but to triumph. Dr. Tony E. Medley Sr. masterfully guides us through Scripture, biblical principles, and Spirit-inspired encouragement that awakens courage and builds resilience. Each chapter shines a light on the truths that sustain the soul: the strength of your heart, the power of your mind, the boldness of your declaration, the assurance of your faith, and the victory that comes through Christ alone.

This book is not written from theory but from lived conviction. It is the voice of one who has walked through life's battles and emerged with a testimony of God's unfailing faithfulness. As you read, you will discover that adversity does not disqualify you—it prepares you. Affliction does not destroy you—it positions you. And faith, when held onto with determination, always leads to abundant victory.

Whether you are weary, questioning, or simply hungry for more of God's power in your life, this book will speak directly to your spirit. It will challenge you to worship deeper, believe stronger, press harder, and never let go of the One who promised, "I will never leave you nor forsake you."

So, as you turn these pages, do not approach them casually. Approach them with expectation. Let the truths soak into your heart. Allow them to ignite fresh passion, unwavering boldness, and unshakable faith.

And above all—remember this one resounding charge: Don't you dare give up.

Part I – Strength for the Journey

1

Hold Fast (Katecho)

Anchored in God's Covenant

> " This is the covenant I will make with them after that time, says the Lord.
> I will put my laws in their hearts, and I will write them on their minds."
> Then he adds: "Their sins and lawless acts I will remember no more."
> ...Let us **hold fast** the profession of our faith without wavering;
> (for he is faithful that promised;)
> — Hebrews 10:16–17, 23

The Covenant Written on the Heart

Every covenant God makes with His people is sealed with His Word. Under the Old Covenant, the law was engraved on stone tablets, distant and external, often reminding Israel of their inability to keep it. But under the New Covenant, through the blood of Christ, God inscribes His truth directly upon the heart of every believer.

This is no small shift—it is the difference between rules etched in cold stone and living truth breathed into warm, beating hearts. What God writes on your heart is not easily erased. He carves His promises into the very core of who you are.

Think of it this way: when the world is loud and distractions surround you, you may forget what someone said to you yesterday. But what God writes on your heart remains. It is a permanent reminder of His will, His grace, and His calling on your life.

And here is the astounding part: God declares that He will "remember your sins no more." The very God who knows all all things chooses to put your failures out of His mind, never again counting them against you. If He has chosen to forget them, why do you keep remembering them?

Drawing Near with Confidence

Verse 22 calls us to "draw near with a true heart in full assurance of faith." In Christ, we no longer stand outside the veil of God's presence, hoping for acceptance. The blood of Jesus tore the veil, opening the way into the very throne room of grace.

To draw near means more than Sunday worship or a whispered prayer before bed. It is an invitation to live daily in close fellowship with God—to bring your worries, hopes, and deepest longings before Him with confidence.

Confidence does not mean arrogance. It means assurance that your Father welcomes you because of Christ's sacrifice. Too many believers live at arm's length from God, afraid He is displeased, uncertain if He will receive them. Hebrews reminds us that because of Jesus, we can approach boldly, not timidly, knowing that His arms are always open.

What It Means to Hold Fast (Katecho)

At the center of this passage lies a powerful command: "Let us hold fast." The Greek word here is Katecho, which means to hold down, to seize, to possess, to keep in memory, and to cling tightly.

To "hold fast" is more than a suggestion; it is a lifeline. Imagine a sailor in a violent storm gripping the ropes of the ship to keep from being thrown overboard. That is the picture of Katecho—gripping God's promises with such tenacity that no storm of doubt, no wave of trial, no gust of fear can pull you away. Holding fast means:

- Holding Down – Subduing the lies of the enemy under the weight of God's truth.
- Keeping in Memory – Rehearsing God's promises so they are not forgotten.
- Making Toward – Pressing forward in hope, even when the path is unclear.
- Possessing – Claiming God's Word as your inheritance, not just theory.
- Seizing On – Refusing to let go of what God has spoken, even in delay.

Faith is not passive. To hold fast is an active, determined, and unrelenting choice.

The Struggle to Keep Your Grip

If we are commanded to "hold fast," it is because life will give us every reason to let go. Doubt creeps in when prayers seem unanswered. Fear rises when circumstances don't shift. Temptation whispers that compromise is easier than obedience.

- Doubt tells you, "God may not come through."

- Discouragement says, "Why bother holding on? It's not working."
- Distraction pulls your focus away from what matters most.
- Deception tries to convince you that something other than God is more reliable.

Peter knew this battle well. When he stepped out of the boat to walk on water, his faith held him up—until the wind distracted him. He looked at the storm instead of Jesus, and he began to sink. Holding fast means keeping your eyes on Christ, no matter how fierce the wind may blow.

Anchored by God's Faithfulness

The good news is that your ability to hold fast does not rest on your strength alone. Verse 23 reminds us: "For He who promised is faithful."

God's promises are not fragile hopes. They are unshakable truths anchored in His character. He cannot lie. He does not forget. He never breaks covenant.

When you feel your grip weakening, remember this: God is not asking you to hold fast to your faith in yourself, but to your faith in Him. And He is faithful.

Think of a child crossing a busy street holding their father's hand. The child may grip weakly, but the father's strong hand ensures they are safe. In the same way, even when your faith falters, God's grip on you never does.

Practical Ways to Hold Fast

How do you live this out in daily life?

1. **Memorize Scripture** – Plant the Word deep in your heart so it rises up when needed.

2. **Speak God's Promises** – Declare His Word aloud; faith grows when you hear it.
3. **Journal God's Faithfulness** – Record answered prayers and moments of His grace.
4. **Surround Yourself with Faith-Builders** – Fellowship with those who encourage you.
5. **Stay in Prayer** – Prayer keeps your heart anchored when storms rage.

Holding fast is not a one-time event. It is a lifestyle of gripping God's Word each day.

Reflection Questions

1. What promise of God are you holding on to right now?
2. When have you been tempted to let go of your faith? What pulled you back?
3. What practical step can you take today to strengthen your grip on God's Word?

Prayer

"Lord, teach me to hold fast to Your promises. When doubts arise, anchor me in Your truth. When fear whispers, remind me of Your faithfulness. When distractions come, fix my eyes on Jesus. Write Your Word deep within my heart and let it guide me each day. I will hold fast, not by my strength, but by Your unfailing hand. Amen."

2

The Covenant

God's Disposition Toward You

When Promises Feel Fragile

One of the hardest things for many people is trusting promises. Perhaps you grew up hearing things that never came to pass:

- "I'll always be there for you."
- "I promise I won't leave."
- "This time, I've really changed."

When promises are broken repeatedly, our hearts develop calluses. We learn to brace ourselves for disappointment. We start to believe that promises are words meant to make us feel better in the moment—but nothing more.

And so when God says, "This is the covenant I will make with you... I will never leave you nor forsake you," our first instinct is often to doubt. What if He changes His mind? What if I fail too badly? What if His patience runs out?

That's why understanding God's covenant is so important. It isn't a fragile promise that can snap under the weight of your mistakes. It's a disposition—a permanent posture of His heart toward you.

The Meaning of Diatheke

In the Greek, the word for covenant is Diatheke. It carries both the sense of a contract and a disposition. That means God isn't simply handing you terms and conditions to sign; He's showing you His heart posture.

Think of it this way: a contract says, "I will do this if you do that." A disposition says, "This is who I am toward you, no matter what."

God's covenant is not based on a shaky "if/then" agreement. It's built on a "because/therefore" foundation:

- Because Christ has given His blood,
- Therefore you are secure in My love.

This is counseling truth for your soul: God's disposition toward you is not moody or unpredictable. His covenant is His steady, faithful heartbeat of love.

Counseling Moment: God's Mood

Let me ask you something: when you picture God's mood toward you right now, what do you see?

- Do you see Him frowning, arms crossed, disappointed in you?
- Do you see Him distant, too busy for your struggles?
- Or do you see Him smiling, arms open, ready to receive you?

So many of us carry an image of God that reflects old wounds from human relationships. If you grew up with a parent who was hard to please, you might assume God is never satisfied either. If you've been abandoned in relationships, you might fear God will eventually walk out too.

But Scripture says His covenant mood toward you is love. Always love. Never shifting with the weather.

Take a moment. Close your eyes if you can. Imagine God looking at you—not with scorn, not with coldness, but with compassion. His disposition toward you is mercy. His heart toward you is steady.

Case Study: Marcus's Story

Marcus grew up in a home where nothing was ever good enough. If he brought home a "B" on his report card, his father wanted to know why it wasn't an "A." If he scored two goals in a game, his coach reminded him of the shots he missed. As an adult, Marcus carried that mindset into his walk with God.

Whenever he stumbled, he imagined God's disappointment. Whenever he prayed, he pictured God rolling His eyes, tired of hearing the same requests. He believed God's mood toward him was irritation.

But then Marcus began to study Hebrews 10. He discovered that covenant meant more than contract. It meant God's permanent disposition of love and mercy. Slowly, he began to replace the image of a scowling father with the reality of a faithful Savior. He learned to rest in God's covenant mood: acceptance.

Maybe, like Marcus, you've been living under the shadow of false assumptions about God's heart. Let His covenant truth counsel your soul today: God's mood toward you is grace.

Practical Counseling Tools

If you struggle to believe God's disposition is steady love, here are some tools:

1. **Covenant Journaling** – Each morning, write down one truth about God's covenant disposition toward you. For example: "Today, God's mood toward me is mercy" (Lamentations 3:22–23). Over time, this re-trains your inner narrative.
2. **Replace the Voice** – Identify whose critical voice you hear when you imagine God's disappointment. Is it a parent? A former partner? Yourself? Then remind your heart: That is not the voice of my Father. His voice speaks grace and truth.
3. **Scripture Meditation** – Choose one covenant verse per week (e.g., Hebrews 13:5, Jeremiah 31:33, John 10:28). Read it daily, speak it aloud, and let it counsel your fears.
4. **Safe Community** – Share your doubts with trusted believers who will remind you of God's covenant love. Sometimes we need someone else to hold up the mirror of truth when our own reflection is cloudy.

Reflection Time

- Who in your past shaped the way you see God's mood?
- What image of God do you most need to let go of?
- How does the idea of God's "disposition" toward you as love bring healing to your story?

Prayer

"Father, I confess that I've often seen You through the lens of my wounds. I've thought of You as distant, critical, or disappointed. But today I choose to believe the truth of Your covenant. Thank You that Your mood toward me is love, that Your disposition is mercy, that Your promises are unbreakable. Heal the places in me that fear abandonment, and anchor me in the safety of Your unchanging heart. Amen."

Part II – Standing Bold in Christ

3

Regulate Your Heart & Mind

The Challenge of Inner Chaos

Have you ever felt like your emotions were running the show? One moment you were hopeful, the next moment discouraged. One day your faith was strong, the next day doubts crept in. Sometimes our hearts and minds seem to swing like a pendulum, never at rest.

Many of us live at the mercy of whatever thoughts and feelings happen to show up. If we wake up anxious, our whole day bends under anxiety's weight. If anger rises, our relationships suffer. If fear whispers, we pull back from opportunities God may be opening.

That's why Scripture calls us to regulate our hearts and minds.

The word regulate means: to bring into conformity with rules, principles, or usage. In other words, we don't let our hearts and minds wander aimlessly. We bring them into alignment with God's truth.

Counseling Picture: A Thermostat vs. a Thermometer

Think of the difference between a thermometer and a thermostat.

- A thermometer only reflects the temperature of the room. If it's hot, the thermometer reads hot. If it's cold, it reads cold. It cannot change anything—it only reacts.

- A thermostat, on the other hand, sets the temperature. It regulates the environment by bringing it into alignment with a standard.

Too many of us live like thermometers—our hearts and minds simply reflect whatever circumstances we face. But God calls us to live like thermostats, regulating our inner world by aligning with His Word.

The Heart and the Mind

The Bible often connects the heart and mind. The heart represents emotions, desires, and motives. The mind represents thoughts, logic, and reasoning. When they are unregulated, they can run wild in opposite directions.

- The heart may chase feelings that are fleeting.
- The mind may spin with anxious thoughts.

When we regulate them under God's principles, they begin to work in harmony:

- The heart rests in God's love.
- The mind trusts in God's truth.

Philippians 4:7 says, "The peace of God, which surpasses all understanding, will guard your hearts and your minds in Christ Jesus." Regulation is about letting God's peace be the guardrail for your inner life.

Case Study: Alicia's Overthinking

Alicia came to counseling exhausted. Her mind never stopped racing. Every decision spun into endless "what ifs." Every mistake replayed in her head like a broken record.

When we explored together, Alicia realized she had no "regulator." Her thoughts ran unchecked, and her emotions followed wherever they led. Through prayer, journaling, and practicing Philippians 4:8—"Think on these things"—she began to retrain her thought life.

It didn't happen overnight, but slowly, Alicia learned to bring her thoughts into conformity with God's truth instead of her fears.

Practical Counseling Tools for Regulation

1. **Breath-Prayer Practice**
   When anxiety rises, practice breathing deeply while repeating a short Scripture truth:
   - Inhale: "The Lord is my Shepherd…"
   - Exhale: "…I shall not want." This calms both body and soul while anchoring you in truth.
2. **Thought Check**
   Ask yourself: "Is this thought true? Is it helpful? Does it align with God's Word?" If not, it needs regulation.
3. **Emotion Naming**
   Instead of saying, "I'm overwhelmed," try, "I feel anxious right now." Naming emotions separates them from your identity and gives space to bring them before God.
4. **Scripture Alignment**
   Write down three Scriptures that counter your most common negative thoughts. Post them where you'll see them daily.

Reflection Time

- Do you tend to live more like a thermometer (reacting) or a thermostat (regulating)?
- What thoughts or emotions most often need regulation in your life?
- Which Scripture can become your "regulating verse" this week?

Prayer

"Lord, I confess that my heart and mind often run unchecked. My thoughts spiral, my emotions overwhelm me, and I lose sight of Your peace. Teach me to regulate my inner world according to Your Word. Help me live as a thermostat, not just a thermometer—setting the tone with truth, not reacting to fear. Guard my heart and my mind in Christ Jesus. Amen."

4

Put: Bringing Forth What God Has Given

The Gift Within

Every person carries something God has "put" inside them. The Greek word Didomi means to give, bring forth, have power, minister. It points to both what God has placed in you and what He calls you to release.

Too often, people sit in counseling rooms feeling empty. They say, "I don't think I have anything to offer." Life's disappointments, comparisons, and failures convince them they are useless. But the truth is, if God has "put" His Spirit in you, then you are not empty. You carry power, gifts, and purpose—even when you feel broken.

Counseling Picture: A Seed in the Soil

Think of a seed buried in the ground. From the outside, it looks small, insignificant, even dead. But inside, life is waiting to burst forth. When the right conditions come—water, sunlight, time—that seed begins to bring forth what was hidden.

The same is true for you. God has put something inside you—spiritual gifts, wisdom, compassion, creativity, leadership, endurance. Maybe it feels buried right now. But buried is not the same as gone. It's waiting to be brought forth.

God Gives for a Purpose

Here's the key: God never gives without purpose. Didomi is not about random distribution. When He gives, He gives intentionally—power to face trials, gifts to build others, compassion to comfort the hurting, wisdom to guide the confused.

1 Corinthians 12 reminds us that spiritual gifts are given "for the common good." That means what God has put in you is not just for you—it's for others. Counseling often uncovers this: healing accelerates when people realize they were not created just to survive but to serve.

Case Study: Elena's Discovery

Elena came to counseling after years of battling depression. She said, "I feel like I have nothing left to give. My life has no meaning."

Over time, Elena began to rediscover a love she once had for encouraging young women. She started writing letters of hope to girls in her church. Slowly, her heart came alive again.

One day she told me, "I realized God put encouragement in me. When I use it, I feel alive. I think this is part of why I'm here."

What Elena discovered is a truth for all of us: what God has put in you is connected to your healing. When you bring it forth, not only do others receive life—you do too.

Practical Counseling Tools

1. **Gift Inventory**

   Write down moments in your life when others said, "You're really good at that," or "That helped me so much." Those affirmations often point to what God has put in you.

2. **Prayer of Availability**

Each morning, pray: "Lord, whatever You have put in me, help me to bring it forth today to bless someone else."

3. **Small Steps of Ministry**

You don't have to wait for a stage or a spotlight. Ministry begins in small acts: a kind word, a listening ear, a helping hand. Every time you use what God has put in you, you are ministering.

4. **Affirmation Journal**

Record every time someone expresses gratitude for something you did or said. Review these moments often—they are reminders that God is bringing forth what He put in you.

Reflection Time

- What do you believe God has "put" in you that may still be buried?
- How have you seen glimpses of your gifts bless others in the past?
- What small step can you take this week to bring forth what God has given you?

Prayer

"Father, thank You for what You have put inside me. Forgive me for the times I've doubted or hidden the gifts You've given. Help me bring forth what You have planted. Show me how to use it with power, with humility, and with love to minister to others. May what You have put in me bring glory to Your name. Amen."

Part III – Drawing Near to God

5

Heart: The Seat of Thoughts and Feelings

The Heart Behind the Smile

Have you ever met someone who smiled outwardly but carried pain inwardly? They laughed at jokes, nodded in conversation, but their eyes told another story. That's because the heart—the inner life of thoughts and feelings—often holds truths our outward expressions cannot hide forever.

The Bible tells us in Proverbs 4:23, "Above all else, guard your heart, for everything you do flows from it." Your heart is not just the place of emotion, but the center of your being—the crossroads where thought and feeling meet. The Greek word Kardia doesn't mean the physical organ; it refers to the core of your mind, motives, and emotions.

In counseling, so much begins with what's in the heart. We can treat surface behaviors, but until the heart is addressed, lasting change rarely comes.

The Inner Dialogue

Your heart is where your private conversations happen. It's where you tell yourself who you are, what you're worth, and what's possible.

- If your heart is filled with lies, your life will follow patterns of fear and defeat.
- If your heart is filled with truth, your life will flow with hope and peace.

Jesus said, "Out of the abundance of the heart the mouth speaks" (Matthew 12:34). In other words, what fills your heart will eventually spill out in your words, choices, and relationships.

Counseling Picture: The Filter of the Heart

Think of your heart like a water filter. Whatever pours through it affects the purity of what comes out. If the filter is clogged with bitterness, then bitterness will leak out. If it's filled with love and truth, then peace and kindness flow more naturally.

That's why regulating and guarding the heart is not about suppressing feelings—it's about tending to the filter. What are you allowing into your heart? What narratives are shaping your thoughts? What voices are you listening to?

Case Study: David's Healing Journey

David came into counseling struggling with anger. Every small frustration at work turned into an outburst. Every disagreement at home led to shouting. At first glance, it seemed like a behavior problem.

But as we dug deeper, we discovered that David's heart was filled with old wounds from rejection. As a child, he often heard, "You'll never be good enough." Those words took root, shaping his inner dialogue. Every challenge felt like another confirmation of that lie, and anger became his defense.

Healing came when David learned to identify those lies and replace them with truth from Scripture: "I am fearfully and wonderfully made"

(Psalm 139:14). Over time, his heart filter changed. And when the heart changed, so did his behavior.

God's Desire for Your Heart

God is not only concerned with outward obedience; He longs for the heart. In Ezekiel 36:26, He promises: "I will give you a new heart and put a new spirit in you."

This means God is not asking you to patch up a broken heart with duct tape. He wants to transform it—replacing lies with truth, fear with love, and shame with acceptance.

Practical Counseling Tools

1. **Heart Journaling**
   Spend five minutes each day writing down the emotions you felt most strongly. Ask: "What thought was connected to that feeling?" This helps you see the heart's patterns.
2. **Truth Replacement**
   For every negative inner dialogue ("I'm not enough," "God has abandoned me"), find a Scripture truth to replace it.
3. **Heart Check Prayer**
   At the end of the day, pray Psalm 139:23–24: "Search me, O God, and know my heart... lead me in the way everlasting."
4. **Emotional Honesty**
   Don't suppress feelings. Bring them into the light of God's presence. Even Jesus wept, grieved, and expressed emotion. Your heart is safe with Him.

Reflection Time

- What words or experiences from your past still shape the thoughts of your heart today?

- When you listen closely to your inner dialogue, does it sound more like God's truth or old lies?
- How would your relationships change if your heart was more at rest in God's love?

Prayer

"Lord, I bring You my heart—my thoughts, my feelings, my inner life. I confess that some of what fills my heart is not from You: old lies, buried wounds, hidden fears. I ask You to cleanse and renew my heart. Guard it with Your peace. Fill it with Your love. And let everything I do flow from a heart that is steady, healed, and anchored in You. Amen."

6

Minds: Deep Thoughts and Understanding

When the Mind Won't Rest

Have you ever lain awake at night while your thoughts ran in circles? Your body was tired, but your mind wouldn't stop rehearsing worries, regrets, or endless "what ifs."

The Greek word Dianoia speaks to these deep, inner workings of the mind. It's more than surface thoughts—it's the underlying disposition that shapes how we process life. It is where understanding is formed.

The mind is powerful. Left unregulated, it can magnify fear, distort truth, and create confusion. But when surrendered to God, the mind becomes a place of clarity, wisdom, and peace.

Counseling Picture: The Well of Deep Thoughts

Imagine your mind as a deep well. Every bucket you draw up from that well shapes your perspective. If the water is polluted—filled with lies, negativity, and fear—then everything you draw up will taste bitter. But if the well is filled with truth, then every thought that rises up brings life and refreshment.

This is why Paul urges us in Romans 12:2: "Be transformed by the renewing of your mind." Renewal means clearing out the polluted waters and letting God fill your well with truth.

The Mind's Disposition

Our dianoia is not just random thoughts—it is the settled disposition of the mind. This is important, because what you think repeatedly becomes how you see the world.

- If your mind's disposition is fear, you will interpret life through fear.
- If it is anger, you will interpret life through anger.
- If it is gratitude, you will interpret life through gratitude.

Counseling often reveals this: two people can face the same situation, yet one sees despair while the other sees hope. The difference is not the circumstance—it's the disposition of the mind.

Case Study: Naomi's Battle with Overthinking

Naomi came into counseling feeling trapped by her own thoughts. She could not stop replaying mistakes from her past. Her mind's disposition was guilt. No matter how much reassurance she received, she always circled back to the belief: "I'll never be good enough."

Over time, Naomi learned to recognize these thought loops for what they were—deep grooves worn into her mind by years of repetition. Together, we worked on practicing Philippians 4:8: "Think on whatever is true, noble, right, pure, lovely, admirable."

At first, it felt unnatural, like trying to redirect a river that had flowed the same way for decades. But slowly, her disposition shifted. Guilt gave way to grace. Her dianoia was being renewed.

God's Desire for Your Mind

Ephesians 4:23 urges us to "be renewed in the spirit of your minds." This renewal is not about emptying your mind, but filling it with God's truth until it reshapes your understanding.

Jesus said the greatest commandment is to "love the Lord your God with all your heart, soul, and mind" (Matthew 22:37). Loving God with your mind means aligning your deep thoughts and understanding with His character. It means letting your inner disposition be shaped by grace instead of fear, by hope instead of despair.

Practical Counseling Tools

1. **Thought Tracing**
   When a negative feeling arises, trace it back: "What thought produced this feeling?" Then trace that thought deeper: "What belief is shaping this thought?" This helps uncover the disposition beneath surface emotions.

2. **Scripture Rewiring**
   Choose one Scripture that counters your deepest recurring negative thought. Write it, memorize it, speak it until it becomes your mind's new disposition.

3. **Renewal Practices**
   - Morning meditation on God's promises.
   - Limiting negative media that fuels fear or anger.
   - Replacing overthinking with gratitude lists.

4. **Counseling Dialogue with God**
   Pray conversationally: "Lord, this is what my mind is telling me. What is Your truth about it?" Wait and listen. Let His Spirit reshape your understanding.

Reflection Time

- What is your mind's current disposition—fear, guilt, anger, peace, gratitude?
- What thoughts dominate your inner world most often?
- What would change in your life if your dianoia was renewed daily by God's Word?

Prayer

"Lord, I give You my mind—the deep thoughts I can't always control, the loops I can't break, the worries that weigh me down. Renew my dianoia. Transform my understanding. Shape my disposition until my mind reflects Your peace and truth. Help me love You not only with my heart, but with the very depths of my mind. Amen."

7

Boldness: Declaring Your Victory in Christ

The Struggle with Boldness

Many people come into counseling weighed down by fear—fear of failure, fear of rejection, fear of being judged. Some even fear approaching God, convinced they are unworthy to come close.

But Hebrews 10:19 gives us a radical truth:

"Having therefore, brothers and sisters, boldness to enter into the Holiest by the blood of Jesus..."

Boldness here doesn't mean arrogance. It means confident freedom of speech—the ability to come before God without shame, and to speak victory over your life because of Christ's finished work.

Counseling Picture: The Locked Door

Imagine standing outside a locked door, hearing laughter, music, and warmth inside—but afraid to knock, because you don't think you belong. That's how many feel about God's presence. They hear about His love, they watch others rejoice, but they hold back, certain they're not welcome.

Boldness means realizing the door is not locked at all. Jesus opened it by His blood. You don't have to wait outside—you are invited in.

Boldness Is Rooted in Identity

The world often tells us boldness comes from personality—being loud, outgoing, or naturally confident. But biblical boldness comes from identity in Christ.

- Without Christ, boldness feels like empty bravado.
- In Christ, boldness is simply walking in what He has already given you.

When you know you are forgiven, chosen, and loved, you no longer shrink back in shame. You declare, "I am victorious because Jesus is victorious."

Case Study: Terrence's Turning Point

Terrence grew up in a home where he was constantly told to "stay quiet" and "don't make waves." By adulthood, those words became a mindset. He avoided speaking up at work, stayed silent in church, and even struggled to pray aloud.

In counseling, we studied Hebrews 10:19 together. Terrence began to see that boldness wasn't about personality—it was about permission. He realized Christ had given him access to God's presence. One day, he prayed aloud for the first time in group counseling. With tears in his eyes, he said afterward, "I never knew I had the right to speak like that."

That was his turning point. Terrence didn't suddenly become loud or flashy—but he became bold in Christ, declaring victory over fear and shame.

Practical Counseling Tools

1. **Victory Declarations**
   Write and speak daily affirmations rooted in Scripture:
   ◦ "By the blood of Jesus, I have access to God."

- "I am more than a conqueror through Him who loves me."
- "The Lord is my helper; I will not fear."

2. **Practice Bold Prayer**

   Instead of whispering silent prayers of survival, practice praying prayers of victory. Speak God's promises aloud, not because He needs to hear them louder, but because your heart does.

3. **Bold Step Exercise**

   Identify one area of life where fear keeps you silent. Take one bold step this week—speak truth in love, share your testimony, or step forward in faith.

4. **Rehearse Grace, Not Shame**

   When shameful thoughts rise up, counter them with bold grace. Say: "Yes, I failed there, but Jesus' blood speaks louder than my failure."

Reflection Time

- Where in your life do you tend to shrink back instead of stepping forward in boldness?
- How would your prayers change if you fully believed you had access to God's presence?
- What declaration of victory do you need to speak over your life today?

Prayer

"Lord, thank You that by the blood of Jesus I can enter Your presence with boldness. Forgive me for the times I have let fear or shame keep me silent. Teach me to boldly declare the victory that is mine in Christ. Let my words, my prayers, and my life reflect confidence—not in myself, but in You. Amen."

8

Boldness: Living with Parresia

What Is Parresia?

The Greek word Parresia means more than confidence. It means an all-outspokenness—the freedom to speak with frankness, honesty, and assurance. In the New Testament, it describes the early believers who, filled with the Holy Spirit, spoke the truth of Christ boldly even when threatened.

For many of us, however, boldness feels unnatural. We fear being too direct. We worry about offending. We hold back our testimony, soften our convictions, or hide our struggles to avoid criticism.

But counseling often reveals this: when we silence ourselves, we shrink. When we speak truth in love, we grow.

Counseling Picture: The Mask We Wear

Think of the masks we put on in daily life. At work, we present ourselves as confident even if we're anxious. At church, we act joyful even when we're hurting. With friends, we laugh along even when we disagree.

Masks feel safe, but they come at a cost. They hide the true self God created and prevent authentic connection.

Parresia invites us to live unmasked—to speak honestly, to bring our full selves into God's presence and into relationships. This is not about rudeness or recklessness; it's about assurance. It is saying, "I don't need to pretend. I can speak truth, because my identity is secure in Christ."

Boldness in Scripture

Acts 4:13 describes the apostles as bold, even though they were "unschooled, ordinary men." Their parresia did not come from education or status, but from being with Jesus.

This is the root of Christian boldness: assurance in Christ's presence, not self-reliance. Boldness is not arrogance—it is authenticity fueled by grace.

Case Study: Marissa's Voice

Marissa entered counseling because she felt invisible. She rarely spoke up at work, even when she had good ideas. At church, she wanted to share her testimony but always froze in fear.

Her turning point came when she realized her silence was rooted in people-pleasing. She was terrified of what others might think.

We studied parresia together. Slowly, she began taking steps—sharing a thought in a meeting, praying aloud in her small group, telling a friend her story of faith.

One day she told me, "For the first time, I feel like I'm living unmasked. I'm not trying to impress anyone; I'm just being who God made me." That's parresia—frankness, assurance, authenticity.

Practical Counseling Tools

1. **Unmasking Exercise**
   Write down three situations where you wear a "mask." Then write what you wish you could say or do if you were truly authentic. Ask God for courage to take one step toward boldness this week.

2. **Truth-Telling Journaling**
   Each day, write one truth you've been afraid to admit—whether about yourself, your feelings, or your faith. Speaking it on paper is a step toward speaking it in life.

3. **Bold Prayer**
   Practice praying with honesty, not formality. Tell God exactly what you feel—joy, anger, fear, hope. Boldness with people begins with boldness in His presence.

4. **Affirmation of Assurance**
   Say aloud: "I have assurance in Christ. I do not need to hide. I can speak truth in love, because my worth is secure in Him."

Reflection Time

- What "masks" do you wear most often, and why?
- In what areas of life do you feel silenced by fear of rejection or judgment?
- What would change if you lived with parresia—frankness, openness, assurance—in your relationships and faith?

Prayer

"Lord, thank You that You invite me to live with parresia—boldness, assurance, and honesty. Forgive me for the times I've hidden behind masks out of fear. Teach me to live unashamed, to speak truth in love, and to walk in the freedom You've given me. Help me declare my faith, share my story, and live authentically, rooted in Your grace. Amen."

9

Turn It Up!!! Drawing Closer in Worship

The Call to Turn It Up

Hebrews 10:22 urges us: "Let us draw near with a true heart in full assurance of faith, having our hearts sprinkled from an evil conscience and our bodies washed with pure water."

To "hold on" in difficult seasons, Scripture says we must draw near. The slide puts it plainly: to hold on, you have to turn up your worship.

Turning it up is not about noise—it's about depth. It's about drawing closer to God than you ever have before.

Counseling Picture: Turning the Dial

Think of an old radio dial. When the signal was weak, you had to turn it just a little higher to tune in. Worship works like that. When life's static grows loud—stress, worry, fear—you need to turn the dial toward God, tuning in closer until His voice becomes clearer.

For some, turning it up may mean lifting hands in praise. For others, it may mean singing louder, kneeling in prayer, journaling honestly, or sitting silently in God's presence. Worship is not about form—it's about focus.

Why Worship Matters in Holding On

When counseling people through seasons of despair, I often see them grow quiet in worship. Pain makes them withdraw. But Scripture teaches the opposite: when life shakes, that's the time to press in deeper.

Worship shifts perspective:

- It takes your eyes off the storm and fixes them on the Savior.
- It reframes problems in the light of God's power.
- It strengthens your spirit by reminding you of who God is.

Worship is not denial of reality—it is declaring a greater reality: God is still faithful.

Case Study: Jonathan's Breakthrough

Jonathan felt spiritually numb. In his words, "I pray, but it feels like talking to a wall. I sing, but the words mean nothing." He was close to giving up altogether.

I encouraged him to "turn it up." Not by forcing more effort, but by drawing closer in honesty. Instead of polished prayers, I told him to pour out raw worship. He began journaling psalms of lament, singing softly through tears, and writing down moments of gratitude each day.

Weeks later he said, "Something broke through. I feel like God is nearer, not because He moved, but because I did." Jonathan discovered that worship is not about performance—it's about proximity.

Practical Counseling Tools

1. **Turn-Up Moments**
   Identify when discouragement creeps in. Instead of withdrawing, practice a quick act of worship—singing, praying, or thanking God.

2. **Honest Worship**
   Bring your true self to God. If you're angry, worship through lament. If you're joyful, worship through praise. Authenticity draws you closer than pretense.
3. **Daily Drawing Near**
   Set aside one daily practice that helps you feel close to God—morning prayer, evening gratitude, Scripture meditation, or quiet reflection.
4. **Worship Playlist**
   Create a playlist of songs that lift your spirit and remind you of God's faithfulness. Play it when your soul feels heavy.

Reflection Time

- What does "turning up your worship" look like for you personally?
- When have you felt closest to God in worship—what helped create that closeness?
- What step could you take this week to draw nearer than ever before?

Prayer

"Lord, I hear Your call to draw near. I confess that sometimes my worship has grown quiet, distant, distracted. Today, I choose to turn it up. Teach me to worship in spirit and truth—not for show, but for closeness. Let my heart, my voice, and my life declare Your greatness. Draw me nearer than I have ever been before. Amen."

Part IV – Endurance Through Trials

10

With a True Heart: Living Unconcealed Before God

The Weight of Pretending

Many people spend years hiding behind spiritual masks. They show up at church smiling, saying "I'm blessed," even when their heart is breaking. They pray polished prayers while hiding raw emotions. They talk about faith but conceal their doubts.

But Hebrews 10:22 calls us to draw near "with a true heart." The Greek word Alethinos means truthful, genuine, unconcealed. A true heart does not mean a perfect heart. It means an honest one.

God is not asking for performance—He's asking for presence.

Counseling Picture: The Hidden Room

Imagine your heart as a house. Most people keep their living room neat for guests, but they have a hidden room where all the clutter gets shoved. That's where the secrets, wounds, and shame are stored.

When guests arrive, the door stays shut. They only see the polished surface.

Too often, we treat God the same way. We let Him into the "clean" parts of our heart but keep the hidden room locked. A true heart opens every door. It says, "God, here is all of me—what I'm proud of and what I'm ashamed of. I'm not concealing anymore."

Why Honesty Heals

Counseling work shows us that healing begins the moment someone says out loud what they've been hiding for years. Secrets lose their power when exposed to light.

Psalm 51:6 says, "You desire truth in the inward being; you teach me wisdom in the secret heart." God longs for honesty—not to shame us, but to heal us.

A true heart draws near not with pretense, but with vulnerability. And vulnerability is where intimacy with God deepens.

Case Study: Lydia's Hidden Fear

Lydia looked like a model believer. She served faithfully, led Bible study, and always seemed strong. But in counseling, she admitted something she had never told anyone: "I'm terrified God will one day decide He's done with me."

That hidden fear shaped her entire spiritual life. She was working to earn God's love, not resting in it.

When she finally brought that fear to God in prayer, she experienced peace she hadn't known before. She told me later, "I thought God wanted me strong. But He wanted me honest." That's the freedom of a true heart—no longer concealing.

Practical Counseling Tools

1. **Honesty Inventory**
   Write down areas of life where you feel pressure to "look fine." Ask: What would it mean to be honest here—with God, with myself, with others?

2. **Unconcealed Prayer**

Practice praying without filters. If you're angry, say it. If you're afraid, admit it. If you're grateful, express it fully. A true heart holds nothing back.

3. **Safe Sharing**

Share one hidden burden with a trusted friend, counselor, or mentor. Speaking it aloud breaks the power of secrecy.

4. **Scripture of Truth**

Meditate on John 8:32: "You shall know the truth, and the truth shall set you free." Let God's truth replace fear and shame.

Reflection Time

- What "hidden room" in your heart do you keep locked away?
- How have masks or pretense kept you from deeper intimacy with God?
- What step can you take this week to live with a truer, more unconcealed heart?

Prayer

"Father, I come before You not with a polished mask, but with a true heart. You see the hidden places I've tried to conceal—the fears, the failures, the wounds. I choose today to bring them into Your light. Teach me that honesty with You leads to healing, not rejection. Help me live with a heart that is genuine, truthful, and fully open to Your love. Amen."

11

In Full Assurance: Living with Entire Confidence

The Struggle with Doubt

For many, faith feels fragile. They believe one moment and question the next. They pray with hope but wrestle with whispers of doubt: "What if God doesn't hear me? What if His promises don't apply to me? What if I'm not truly forgiven?"

Counseling often uncovers this tug-of-war inside people's hearts. Faith is present, but it is shaky—constantly battling uncertainty. That is why Hebrews 10:22 calls us to draw near to God "in full assurance of faith."

The Greek word Plerophoria means entire confidence. It paints the picture of a faith so steady that doubt no longer dominates. It is not blind optimism, but confidence rooted in a trustworthy relationship with God.

Counseling Picture: The Chair You Trust

Think of sitting in a chair. When you believe it will hold you, you don't test it with hesitation—you sit with your full weight. That's what full assurance looks like.

Many believers "perch" on their faith, half-sitting, half-holding themselves up, afraid it might not hold. But Plerophoria is leaning your full weight into God, trusting that He will not fail.

Confidence in Relationship

Confidence in God is not arrogance; it's relationship. Verse 22 reminds us that assurance flows from hearts sprinkled clean and consciences freed. In other words, we don't build confidence by pretending we are flawless. We build it by trusting that Christ's sacrifice has made us secure. Confidence grows in any relationship when two things are present:

1. Consistency – showing up daily with honesty.
2. Trustworthiness – knowing the other will keep their word.

God has proven His consistency and trustworthiness throughout Scripture and in our lives. Our part is to draw near, again and again, until confidence replaces doubt.

Case Study: Michael's Fear of Failing God

Michael came into counseling convinced that God was disappointed in him. He said, "I feel like God is always just one step away from giving up on me."

This belief left him insecure in prayer, hesitant in worship, and fearful of the future. Together we studied Hebrews 10 and the meaning of Plerophoria. Slowly, Michael realized that God's covenant love was not fragile. It wasn't based on his performance but on Christ's finished work.

One session, with tears in his eyes, he said, "For the first time, I feel like I can breathe. I don't have to wonder every day if God loves me. I just know." That is the fruit of full assurance—freedom from doubt in a trustful relationship.

Practical Counseling Tools

1. **Confidence Confessions**
   Speak daily: "I have full assurance in Christ. I am loved, forgiven, and secure."
2. **Faith Chair Exercise**
   When you face fear, visualize yourself sitting fully in the "chair" of God's promises. Say aloud: "I put my full weight on You, Lord."
3. **Trust Journal**
   Record times when God has proven faithful—answered prayers, unexpected provision, peace in hard moments. Review them when doubt rises.
4. **Scripture Anchors**
   Memorize verses of assurance: Hebrews 10:22, 1 John 5:13, Philippians 1:6. Use them as anchors when insecurity threatens.

Reflection Time

- Where do you struggle most with doubt—in prayer, in forgiveness, in daily trust?
- How does the picture of sitting fully in a chair help you understand assurance?
- What steps can you take to grow confidence in your relationship with God this week?

Prayer

"Father, thank You that You call me to live in full assurance. I confess that doubt often shakes me, and fear whispers that I am not enough.

But today I choose to rest my full weight on You. Teach me to trust Your Word, to lean into Your love, and to live with entire confidence in Christ. Let my faith be steady, not shaken. Amen."

12

Of Faith!!!

Living with Persuasion and Reliance on Christ

Faith Beyond Words

Many people say they "have faith," but in counseling, I often ask: "What does that look like in your daily life?" For some, faith is just a word they associate with religion. For others, it's an abstract belief that God exists.

But biblical faith—Pistis—is much more than that. It is persuasion, a deep conviction that moves from the mind to the heart and into action. It is not simply believing about God—it is relying on God.

Faith is not just something you say you have. Faith is the way you live when storms come, when prayers delay, when answers seem far away.

Counseling Picture: The Bridge of Trust

Imagine standing before a bridge that stretches across a deep canyon. You can study the bridge, admire its design, and even say out loud, "I believe this bridge can hold me." But faith is not proven until you step onto the bridge and let your weight rest on it.

Faith in Christ is like that. It's more than acknowledging He can save—it's stepping onto the bridge, entrusting your whole life to Him. Pistis means reliance, not just agreement.

Persuasion of the Heart

The word Pistis also means persuasion. This is important, because life will constantly try to persuade you in the opposite direction.

- Fear will try to persuade you that God won't come through.
- Culture will try to persuade you to rely on yourself.
- Past failures will try to persuade you that you're disqualified.

Faith is letting God's Word be the loudest persuasion in your life. Romans 10:17 reminds us: "Faith comes by hearing, and hearing by the Word of God." The more you hear and rehearse His promises, the stronger your persuasion grows.

Case Study: Sophia's Reliance Shift

Sophia came into counseling burned out. She was juggling work, family, ministry, and life responsibilities, relying on her own strength to keep it all together. She said, "I believe in God, but I feel like everything depends on me."

Over time, Sophia learned that faith meant reliance—not just on her ability, but on Christ's sufficiency. She began surrendering her daily burdens in prayer: "Lord, I can't carry this alone. I rely on You."

She described the shift this way: "I still have responsibilities, but I no longer feel like I'm holding up the world. Faith means I'm not the bridge—He is."

Faith as Moral Conviction

Another dimension of Pistis is moral conviction. Faith shapes not only what you believe but how you live. It means trusting God enough to obey Him even when it's costly.

- Abraham showed faith when he left his homeland, not knowing where God was leading.
- Noah showed faith when he built the ark before a drop of rain had fallen.
- The early church showed faith when they declared Christ in the face of persecution.

Faith says, "I believe so strongly in who God is that I will live differently because of it."

Practical Counseling Tools

1. **Reliance Check**
   Write down three areas of life where you are tempted to rely more on yourself than on Christ. Pray specifically: "Lord, I release this into Your hands."
2. **Persuasion Practice**
   Each day, declare one truth that persuades your heart toward faith: "God is faithful. God is with me. God's promises are true."
3. **Bridge Step**
   Identify one area where you've been standing at the edge of the "bridge," hesitant to trust. Take one small step of obedience that shows reliance.
4. **Faith Journal**
   Keep a record of how God shows up when you trust Him. Over time, this journal becomes evidence that strengthens your persuasion.

Reflection Time

- Where are you still trying to rely on yourself instead of Christ?
- What voices (fear, culture, past wounds) try to persuade you away from faith?
- What would living with moral conviction—faith in action—look like this week?

Prayer

"Lord, thank You for the gift of faith. Teach me to move beyond words into persuasion, conviction, and reliance. Help me to step fully onto the bridge of trust, leaning all my weight on You. Strengthen my heart when fear tries to persuade me otherwise. Let my life show not only what I believe, but whom I rely on. Amen."

13

Sprinkled: Rendered Clean and Made New

The Stains We Carry

Life has a way of leaving stains on us. Guilt from past mistakes. Shame from hidden secrets. Regret over missed opportunities. For many, counseling reveals a deep sense of unworthiness—not just that they've done wrong, but that something inside them feels permanently "unclean."

Hebrews 10:22 gives hope: "Let us draw near... having our hearts sprinkled from an evil conscience."

The Greek word Rhantizo means to render, to cause to become. It's not just about covering up guilt; it's about transformation. When God sprinkles your heart, He doesn't just wash the surface—He renders you clean, causing you to become new.

Counseling Picture: The Stained Garment

Picture a white shirt stained with deep ink. No matter how much you scrub, the stain won't come out. Many live like that—trying harder, scrubbing with guilt, but never feeling clean.

God's sprinkling is not human effort—it's divine action. It's as if the stain is not just removed but the fabric itself is made new. What was once ruined is rendered whole again.

The Power of Render

The word "render" means to cause something to become. That's the heart of grace. God doesn't just declare you forgiven—He causes you to become clean, righteous, whole.

- From guilt to freedom.
- From shame to acceptance.
- From unworthy to beloved.

You don't have to live stained when God has rendered you clean.

Case Study: Daniel's Breakthrough

Daniel carried years of guilt over choices he made in his youth. He believed he was forgiven, but he still felt unclean. Every time he tried to pray, his conscience whispered, "You don't belong here."

In counseling, we studied Hebrews 10 together. When he learned that Rhantizo means "to render, to cause to become," it shifted his perspective. He said, "So I'm not just forgiven in theory—I'm actually made clean in reality."

That breakthrough changed his prayer life. Instead of approaching God in shame, he came with boldness. Daniel realized that God had already rendered him new.

Practical Counseling Tools

1. **Stain List**
   Write down the "stains" you feel from your past—regrets, sins,

failures. Then write across them: "Rendered clean by the blood of Christ."

2. **Sprinkling Prayer**

Each morning, pray: "Lord, sprinkle my heart again today. Render me clean. Cause me to become who You've already declared I am."

3. **Scripture Bath**

Read and meditate on cleansing Scriptures (Hebrews 9:14, 1 John 1:7, Isaiah 1:18). Let them wash over your conscience.

4. **Shift from Trying to Trusting**

Stop trying to "scrub yourself clean" with effort. Instead, trust that Christ has already rendered you clean by His sacrifice.

Reflection Time

- What "stains" from your past do you still carry in your conscience?
- How does the idea of God rendering you clean (not just forgiving, but transforming) change how you see yourself?
- What would it look like to live as though you are already clean in Christ?

Prayer

"Lord, thank You that through Christ I have been sprinkled—rendered clean from an evil conscience. I confess that I sometimes still live as though I'm stained, but today I receive Your transforming grace. Cause me to become what You already see in me: forgiven, cleansed, and whole. Let me live boldly in the freedom of being made new. Amen."

14

I'm Going to Hold On Until My Change Comes

When Change Feels Delayed

Few things test faith like waiting. You pray, you believe, you try to stay hopeful — but the situation doesn't shift. Bills still stack up. The doctor's report still says the same thing. The child still hasn't come home.

In moments like these, many are tempted to give up, assuming God has forgotten. But Hebrews 10:23 speaks directly to that temptation: "Let us hold fast... without wavering; for He is faithful that promised."

God doesn't tell us to hold fast because the wait will be easy. He tells us to hold fast because His faithfulness guarantees the promise, even if the timing stretches us.

Counseling Picture: The Knot in the Rope

Imagine hanging from a rope over a cliff. Your arms grow weak, your grip slips. But there's a knot tied near the end. You grab onto that knot and hold on with everything you've got.

That knot is God's faithfulness. When you feel like letting go, the knot keeps you secure. Holding fast doesn't mean you never feel weak. It means you cling to His promise until your change comes.

The Profession of Faith

Hebrews 10:23 also speaks of holding fast to the profession of our faith. That word means public declaration. In other words, your faith is not just what you believe in your heart—it's what you continue to declare with your mouth, even when circumstances seem unchanged.

- Faith says: "God is my provider," even when money is tight.
- Faith says: "God is my healer," even when symptoms linger.
- Faith says: "God is working," even when the evidence is invisible.

Declaring your faith doesn't deny reality—it proclaims God's greater reality.

Case Study: Elaine's Season of Waiting

Elaine had been praying for reconciliation with her estranged daughter for years. Every holiday was a reminder of absence. She admitted in counseling, "Sometimes I feel like my prayers are hitting the ceiling."

We studied Hebrews 10:23 together. I encouraged her to create a daily declaration of faith, not based on what she saw, but on God's promise. She began speaking aloud each morning: "Lord, You are faithful to heal my family."

Months passed with no visible change. But then, unexpectedly, her daughter called. Reconciliation didn't happen overnight, but a door cracked open. Elaine said, "If I had given up one week earlier, I would've missed it. Holding on really does matter."

Practical Counseling Tools

1. **Faith Declarations**
   Write one statement of faith rooted in Scripture that declares God's promise over your situation. Speak it daily until it becomes stronger than your doubt.
2. **Knot Reminder**
   When you feel like giving up, visualize that knot at the end of the rope—God's faithfulness. Whisper, "He is faithful that promised."
3. **Waiting Journal**
   Record prayers and track small signs of God's movement. Often, change is gradual, but journaling helps you notice His hand at work.
4. **Support in Community**
   Share your profession of faith with a trusted friend or group who can remind you of God's faithfulness when you're tempted to waver.

Reflection Time

- What promise from God are you currently holding onto?
- Where do you feel tempted to waver?
- How could declaring your faith out loud strengthen your endurance in waiting?

Prayer

"Lord, I choose today to hold fast without wavering. Even when change feels delayed, I will trust Your timing. Even when my strength feels weak, I will cling to Your faithfulness. Render my heart steady in the waiting. I refuse to give up until my change comes. For You are faithful who promised. Amen."

Part V – Living in Victory

15

The Conqueror in You

From Survivor to Conqueror

Many people see themselves as survivors. They've made it through pain, betrayal, disappointment, or loss. And survival is important — but survival is not the end goal.

Romans 8:37 says: "In all these things we are more than conquerors through him that loved us."

Notice the phrase "in all these things." The verse doesn't say we conquer by avoiding challenges, but by walking through them with victory. Survival says, "I made it out alive." Conquering says, "I came out stronger, transformed, and victorious."

Counseling Picture: The Inner Warrior

Picture a soldier who has been through battle. The armor is dented, the body is tired, but the soldier still stands — not just surviving, but stronger because of the fight.

That's what being a conqueror looks like. The conqueror in you is not defined by what you went through, but by the Christ who carried you through.

The Difference Between Trying and Trusting

In counseling, I often meet people who feel like they are constantly fighting battles in their own strength. They are exhausted, worn out, and discouraged.

But the truth of Scripture is this: you are not a conqueror because of your willpower, but because of His power. Victory doesn't come from trying harder, but from trusting deeper.

- Without Christ: battles overwhelm.
- With Christ: battles refine and reveal the conqueror inside.

Case Study: Jerome's Discovery

Jerome came into counseling defeated. His business had failed, his marriage was struggling, and he said, "I feel like a loser in every area of my life."

We studied Romans 8 together. I asked him to underline the words, "more than conquerors." I explained that this wasn't about external success, but internal victory.

Slowly, Jerome shifted. Instead of focusing on what he lost, he began focusing on what God was building in him through the losses. He said later, "I thought being a conqueror meant winning battles out there. Now I see it means Christ is winning battles in here."

Practical Counseling Tools

1. **Victory Identity Statement**
   Write: "I am more than a conqueror through Christ who loves me." Post it somewhere visible. Speak it daily until it shapes how you see yourself.
2. **Conqueror Journal**
   Record battles you've faced and how God has carried you

through. Looking back will remind you that victory has always been His pattern.

3. **Shift from Surviving to Thriving**

   Ask: "Am I just surviving, or am I conquering?" Then list steps that move you from survival to victory (gratitude, prayer, declaration, perseverance).

4. **Celebrate Small Wins**

   Conquering doesn't always mean massive victories. Sometimes it means choosing joy today, forgiving someone, or resisting despair. Celebrate every win.

Reflection Time

- Where have you seen yourself more as a survivor than a conqueror?
- What inner battles are you still fighting that Christ wants to turn into victory?
- How would your outlook change if you fully embraced the conqueror inside of you?

Prayer

"Lord, thank You that through Christ I am more than a conqueror. I confess that too often I've lived as if I'm barely surviving. Today, I embrace the conqueror in me—not by my strength, but by Your Spirit. Render me strong, victorious, and unshaken, no matter what I face. Help me walk each day in the confidence of Your love. Amen."

16

Adversity Will Come: Standing Strong in the Storm

Expecting the Storms

One of the hardest things for many believers is the shock of adversity. We ask: "Why me? Why now? Why this?" But Scripture never promises a life without trouble. In fact, Jesus said plainly in John 16:33: "In this world you will have trouble. But take heart! I have overcome the world."

Adversity is not a sign that God has abandoned you. It is part of the human experience. The question is not if adversity will come, but when—and how you will respond when it does.

Counseling Picture: Weatherproof Faith

Think of a house built in a storm-prone region. If the builder knows storms are coming, they don't skimp on the foundation or materials. They prepare the house to endure.

Life works the same way. If we expect adversity, we can prepare our hearts with faith, prayer, and community support. That way, when storms hit, our foundation in Christ keeps us from collapsing.

The Nature of Adversity

Adversity takes many forms:

- Misfortune — sudden loss, financial strain, unexpected sickness.
- Affliction — emotional pain, grief, broken relationships, betrayal.
- Opposition — spiritual battles, criticism, resistance to your calling.

Each form of adversity feels different, but the impact is the same: it tests your resolve to keep holding on.

Case Study: Angela's Storm

Angela lost her job suddenly after 20 years with the same company. She came into counseling overwhelmed with fear about the future. "I don't know how to start over at my age," she said.

We acknowledged the reality of adversity — it was not denial to admit she was in a storm. But then we shifted to hope: reminding her that adversity is never the final word. Together, we created a plan of faith-filled action steps: daily prayer declarations, practical job searches, and leaning on supportive community.

Months later, Angela not only found new work but said, "The storm taught me I was stronger than I thought. And God was more faithful than I imagined."

How to Face Adversity Without Giving Up

1. **Name It Honestly**
   Denial makes adversity heavier. Admit what you're facing, like David in the Psalms: raw, honest, real.

2. **Anchor in Scripture**
   Write down promises like Isaiah 41:10 ("Fear not, for I am with you") and return to them daily.
3. **Lean Into Community**
   Isolation magnifies adversity. Invite trusted friends, pastors, or counselors to walk with you.
4. **Reframe the Battle**
   Instead of asking "Why me?" ask "What is God building in me through this?" Adversity refines faith.
5. **See the End Beyond the Present**
   James 1:2–4 reminds us that trials produce perseverance, maturity, and strength. Adversity doesn't last forever—but it leaves you stronger.

Reflection Time

- What adversity are you currently facing, and how are you interpreting it?
- Do you see storms as punishment, or as opportunities for God's faithfulness to shine?
- What practical step can you take today to prepare or strengthen your foundation against adversity?

Prayer

"Lord, I acknowledge that adversity will come, and I confess that it often shakes me. But I thank You that storms don't have the final word—You do. Teach me to stand strong, to anchor in Your promises, and to lean into Your presence when affliction comes. Render me steadfast so that no adversity can cause me to give up. Amen."

17

Afflictions: God's Deliverance in Every Trial

Facing the Reality of Afflictions

Psalm 34:19 doesn't sugarcoat life: "Many are the afflictions of the righteous." Notice, it doesn't say "some." It says many. Following Christ doesn't insulate us from pain, hardship, or opposition. In fact, the righteous often encounter more afflictions because they are swimming upstream against the currents of a broken world.

But the verse doesn't end there. It continues: "But the LORD delivereth him out of them all." The promise is not that afflictions won't come, but that they won't have the last word. Deliverance is always on the horizon.

Counseling Picture: The Dark Tunnel

Imagine walking through a long, dark tunnel. Affliction feels like that—enclosed, disorienting, endless. But Psalm 34:19 promises there is always an exit. No matter how long the tunnel feels, the light of God's deliverance is ahead.

Affliction is temporary. God's deliverance is permanent.

What Afflictions Look Like

- Physical afflictions — illness, pain, exhaustion.
- Emotional afflictions — grief, depression, anxiety.
- Spiritual afflictions — temptation, opposition, doubt.
- Relational afflictions — betrayal, family strife, isolation.

Every believer faces these in different seasons. But every believer also carries the promise: God will deliver.

Case Study: Thomas's Season of Pain

Thomas was diagnosed with a chronic illness. He said in counseling, "I feel like I'm drowning in affliction. I pray for healing, but the pain doesn't leave."

We studied Psalm 34:19 together. Thomas realized deliverance doesn't always mean immediate removal—it can also mean God giving strength to endure, grace to overcome, and peace that carries you through.

Months later, Thomas said, "The pain hasn't vanished, but God has delivered me from despair. I no longer see affliction as my prison—I see it as my classroom."

The Promise of Deliverance

God's deliverance doesn't always look like instant escape. Sometimes it comes through:

- Strength to endure until the trial passes.
- Wisdom to grow in the middle of the pain.
- Freedom from despair even while circumstances remain.
- Complete release when God turns the page and brings victory.

The key is this: affliction will not define your story. Deliverance will.

Practical Counseling Tools

1. **Affliction Inventory**
   Write down the afflictions weighing on you right now. Next to each, write: "The Lord will deliver me out of this."
2. **Tunnel Visualization**
   When overwhelmed, picture yourself in a tunnel with light at the end. Pray: "Lord, lead me through until I reach deliverance."
3. **Affliction Journal**
   Record ways God has delivered you in the past. Use this as evidence to fuel hope when current trials feel endless.
4. **Daily Declaration**
   Speak aloud: "Many are my afflictions, but the Lord delivers me out of them all."

Reflection Time

- What current affliction feels overwhelming to you?
- How have you seen God deliver you from past afflictions?
- What does "deliverance" look like for you today—strength, wisdom, peace, or release?

Prayer

"Lord, I thank You that even though many are the afflictions of the righteous, You promise to deliver me from them all. Teach me not to lose heart when afflictions press in. Strengthen me to endure, open my eyes to Your presence in the trial, and remind me that deliverance is certain because You are faithful. Amen."

18

Delivereth: The God Who Snatches You Out

The God Who Intervenes

Psalm 34:19 told us that though afflictions are many, "the LORD delivereth him out of them all." The word "delivereth" here is natsal—a strong verb meaning to snatch away, to defend, to cause escape without fail.

This isn't a passive deliverance. It's not God standing by with gentle encouragement. It is God moving decisively to rescue His child. Like a parent rushing to snatch a toddler out of traffic, God's love compels Him to act swiftly and powerfully on your behalf.

Counseling Insight: Rescued Without Fail

Many people in counseling express fear that their situation is beyond saving. They ask:

- "What if God doesn't show up this time?"
- "What if my mistakes disqualify me from deliverance?"
- "What if this affliction is too strong?"

But natsal erases those doubts. It means God's deliverance comes without fail. His timing may stretch us, but His rescue is certain.

A Personal Story

Maria came to counseling after surviving an abusive relationship. She said: "I felt trapped. I prayed for years, wondering if God even heard me. Then, one day, everything shifted. God opened a door of escape I never imagined, and I walked through it."

Looking back, Maria said: "God didn't just encourage me to leave. He snatched me out and defended me when I was at my weakest."

That's natsal. That's the God who delivers.

The Defender at Your Side

Deliverance also carries the meaning of defending. God doesn't just pull you out of trouble — He stands guard so the enemy can't drag you back in.

Think of Israel leaving Egypt. God didn't just deliver them through the Red Sea. He defended them by drowning Pharaoh's army. His deliverance was total — no chance of return.

That same God still works today.

Practical Counseling Applications

1. **Name Your Trap**
   What situation do you feel trapped in? Write it down. Then declare: "God will natsal me out of this."

2. **Look Back at Escapes**
   Remember times when you should have been destroyed — but weren't. Each is proof that God has already snatched you away before, and He will do it again.

3. **Pray the Word**

   Each morning, say: "Lord, deliver me. Snatch me out of the enemy's trap. Defend me. Cause me to escape without fail."

4. **Visualize the Rescue**

   Picture yourself being snatched out of danger by God's strong hand. Let that image strengthen your faith when fear whispers that you are stuck.

Reflection Questions

- What "trap" feels impossible to escape right now?
- How does knowing that God promises to "deliver without fail" change your outlook?
- Do you struggle to believe that God is willing to defend you personally?

Prayer

"Lord, You are my Deliverer. Thank You for being the God who snatches me out of traps, who defends me when I am weak, and who causes me to escape without fail. Strengthen my faith to trust Your timing and Your power. Even when afflictions press me, I will not give up — because You will deliver me. Amen."

19

Victory: The End of the Struggle

The Promise of Victory

Victory is more than winning—it is the completion of a struggle, the final note after a long song of pain. By definition, victory assumes there was a battle. You cannot have victory without struggle. You cannot celebrate triumph without first having endured the contest.

For the believer, every struggle is moving toward a promised ending: victory in Christ.

1 Corinthians 15:57 declares: "But thanks be to God, which giveth us the victory through our Lord Jesus Christ."

Notice—it is not our fight alone. It is His victory given to us.

Counseling Insight: Victory After the Fight

In counseling sessions, many people sit with tears running down their face, asking, "Why does life have to be this hard?"

The truth is, struggles are part of the process toward victory. Without them, we wouldn't know the depth of God's power or the sweetness of His triumph.

- Struggles expose our weakness.
- Battles test our endurance.

- Trials reveal our faith.
- Victory proves God's faithfulness.

The successful ending is not about you being strong enough—it is about God being faithful enough.

A Testimony of Victory

James battled addiction for years. He said: "Every time I tried to quit, I failed. I felt like victory was for everyone else but me."

In time, James came to understand that victory wasn't his to earn—it was his to receive. Through support, prayer, and surrender, he began to walk in freedom.

Looking back, he said: "Victory didn't come the moment I stopped struggling. It came the moment I realized the fight belonged to God, not me."

Victory in Scripture

- Exodus 14:13–14 – "The LORD shall fight for you, and ye shall hold your peace."
- Romans 8:37 – "Nay, in all these things we are more than conquerors through him that loved us."
- 1 John 5:4 – "For whatsoever is born of God overcometh the world: and this is the victory that overcometh the world, even our faith."

Practical Counseling Applications

1. **Name the Contest**
   What is the "contest" in your life right now—fear, doubt, addiction, financial strain, grief? Naming the battle helps prepare you for the victory.

2. **Visualize the End**
Picture yourself at the successful ending. What does life look like after this struggle? Hold that vision close—it fuels endurance.
3. **Victory Journal**
Record past victories, big or small. Every one is proof that God has fought for you before and will do it again.
4. **Declare the Outcome**
Speak this daily: "My struggle will end in victory because my God never loses."

Reflection Questions

- How do you usually feel in the middle of a struggle—discouraged, hopeful, or defeated?
- What does "victory" look like for you in this season?
- Do you believe that God has already secured the ending, even if you're still in the middle?

Prayer

"Lord, thank You that every struggle I face is moving toward victory. Thank You that through Jesus, I am more than a conqueror. Remind me when I feel weak that the battle is Yours, and the ending has already been written. I will not give up, because my story ends in victory. Amen."

20

Believe: The Power of Possibility

The Challenge of Belief

Jesus' words in Mark 9:23 are as direct as they are life-changing: "If thou canst believe, all things are possible to him that believeth."

Belief is not passive—it is active trust, a decision of the heart and mind to accept God's promises as true even when circumstances scream otherwise.

Many give up not because God has failed, but because they stop believing before the breakthrough arrives. This chapter is about refusing to let unbelief rob you of God's possibilities.

Counseling Insight: The Battle of Unbelief

Often in counseling, I've heard:

- "I know God can, but I don't know if He will for me."
- "I've prayed so long, but nothing has changed."
- "I'm afraid to hope again."

Unbelief doesn't always shout—it whispers. It sneaks into our thoughts, convincing us that possibility belongs to everyone else but us.

But Jesus counters those whispers with this truth: "All things are possible to him that believeth."

A Story of Restored Belief

Linda had prayed for her estranged son for years. Her belief weakened with every unanswered phone call. She said: "I wanted to give up. I didn't believe reconciliation was possible anymore."

Through prayer and encouragement, Linda began to choose belief again—not belief in her son's behavior, but belief in God's ability. Months later, her son called. Healing began.

Linda said: "Belief didn't make everything easy, but it kept me standing long enough to see God work."

Belief Opens the Door

Belief doesn't create the miracle—God does. But belief opens the door for His power to flow.

- Abraham believed God, and it was counted as righteousness (Romans 4:3).
- The woman with the issue of blood believed if she touched Jesus' garment, she would be healed (Mark 5:28).
- Blind Bartimaeus believed Jesus could restore his sight and received his miracle (Mark 10:51–52).

Belief positions us to receive.

Practical Counseling Applications

1. **Belief Confession**
   Each day, speak aloud: "I believe all things are possible with God."

2. **Doubt Inventory**

Write down the doubts that whisper to you. Next to each, write a Scripture that counters it.

3. **Belief Practice**

Take one area of your life that feels impossible. Each time fear rises, declare: "This is possible with God."

4. **Belief Partner**

Share your struggle with a trusted friend or counselor who can remind you to keep believing when your faith feels weak.

Reflection Questions

- Where in your life do you struggle most to believe?
- What would change if you chose to believe God's word above your feelings?
- Who can you invite to stand with you in belief during this season?

Prayer

"Lord, strengthen my belief. Help me to silence the whispers of doubt and hold tightly to Your promises. I choose to believe that all things are possible with You. Where unbelief has held me back, break its power. Teach me to keep believing. even when the answer hasn't come yet. Amen."

21

Believeth: Trusting God with Your Whole Being

From Belief to Believeth

In the last chapter, we reflected on Mark 9:23 where Jesus said, "If thou canst believe, all things are possible to him that believeth."

Notice the progression. Believe is the initial act of faith. Believeth is the continuing lifestyle of faith — an ongoing trust in God's ability, day after day. It isn't a one-time choice; it's a way of living.

Believeth is choosing to wake up each morning and say, "God, I place my life in Your hands again."

Counseling Insight: The Struggle to Trust

Many people wrestle not with believing that God can do something, but with trusting Him with their well-being.

- "I know God is powerful, but will He take care of me?"
- "I trust Him with eternity, but I struggle to trust Him with my daily needs."
- "I believe He loves others, but sometimes I doubt He loves me enough to act."

Believeth speaks directly to these struggles. It means you not only ac-knowledge God's ability — you rest your life on it.

A Story of Learning to Believeth

Marcus had a high-paying job but lived with constant anxiety. He said: "I believe God exists, but I don't really trust Him with my life. I feel like I have to hold everything together."

Through prayer and counseling, Marcus began practicing believeth. He started releasing small things to God—his schedule, his decisions, his fears. Over time, the anxiety lessened, replaced by peace.

Marcus later said: "Believing God was easy. Believeth—actually trusting Him with my well-being—changed everything."

Scripture Insight

- Proverbs 3:5–6 – "Trust in the LORD with all thine heart; and lean not unto thine own understanding. In all thy ways acknowl-edge him, and he shall direct thy paths."
- John 11:40 – "Said I not unto thee, that, if thou wouldest believe, thou shouldest see the glory of God?"
- Romans 10:10 – "For with the heart man believeth unto right-eousness; and with the mouth confession is made unto salvation."

Believeth connects trust, obedience, and well-being into a complete walk of faith.

Practical Counseling Applications

1. Trust Exchange
   Write down three areas of life you've struggled to release to God (finances, health, relationships, etc.). Pray over each, saying: "Lord, I trust You with this."

2. Daily Believeth Prayer

   Each morning, declare: "Today, I trust God with my life, my needs, and my future."

3. Faith Anchors

   Keep reminders of past victories where God cared for you. These anchors strengthen ongoing trust.

4. Release Practice

   Whenever anxiety rises, pause and say: "I choose to believeth—God, I trust You with this moment."

Reflection Questions

- What part of your life is hardest to trust God with?
- How would your stress change if you fully entrusted your well-being to Him?
- What daily practice can you start to shift from belief to believeth?

Prayer

"Lord, I thank You for the gift of faith. Teach me not just to believe in You, but to live in believeth—to trust You with my whole being. I surrender my fears, my needs, and my future into Your hands. Strengthen my trust daily, and help me walk in peace, knowing You are faithful to care for me. Amen."

Part VI – Pressing Toward the Prize

22

Exercise Kingdom Authority

Walking in the Power of Belief

From Belief to Authority

Jesus didn't intend for belief to remain quiet or hidden. In Mark 16:17, He declared that signs would follow those who believe. Faith produces authority, and authority produces evidence.

When you believe, you don't just receive peace for yourself—you carry power to impact the world around you.

Counseling Insight: Authority Feels Unfamiliar

In counseling, many believers confess:

- "I believe in Jesus, but I don't feel powerful."
- "I don't know how to exercise authority."
- "I'm afraid of spiritual warfare."

The truth is, authority doesn't come from feelings—it comes from identity. If you belong to Christ, His authority belongs to you.

What Authority Looks Like

According to Mark 16:17, authority expresses itself in at least two ways:

1. Deliverance: "In my name shall they cast out devils." Believers are equipped to confront darkness and free others from oppression.
2. Empowerment: "They shall speak with new tongues." This symbolizes empowerment by the Spirit, equipping believers to live and minister beyond natural ability.

Authority is not arrogance. It's walking in confidence that God's name carries power greater than any opposition.

Story: Anna's Discovery

Anna grew up in church but always felt powerless in the face of fear. One night, plagued by nightmares, she remembered Mark 16:17. She whispered, "In the name of Jesus, I command fear to leave."

Peace filled the room. For the first time, Anna realized authority was not for "special Christians"—it was for all who believe.

Practical Counseling Applications

1. Identity Affirmation
   Each morning, declare: "I am a believer. Signs will follow me today."
2. Authority Practice
   The next time fear, anxiety, or temptation rises, speak out loud: "In the name of Jesus, leave."
3. Spirit Empowerment
   Ask the Holy Spirit daily to fill you afresh, reminding you that authority is exercised in His power, not your own strength.

4. Help Others
Begin to pray with boldness for family or friends, not timidly but in the confidence of Christ's authority.

Reflection Questions

- Do you struggle to see yourself as someone who carries Kingdom authority? Why?
- How would your daily life change if you truly walked in the authority Jesus gave you?
- What "signs" would you like to see follow your faith?

Prayer

"Lord Jesus, thank You for giving me authority in Your name. Teach me to walk boldly, not in my own strength but in Your power. Let signs follow my life, so that others may see Your glory. Strengthen me to cast out fear, stand against darkness, and walk daily in the fullness of Your Spirit. Amen."

23

Overcomer: Living Out the Victory of Faith

Born to Overcome

John tells us plainly: "Whatsoever is born of God overcometh the world." That means if you are born again, overcoming is not optional—it is your inheritance.

To overcome means to conquer, to prevail, to rise above pressure, temptation, or opposition. And according to this verse, the fuel of overcoming is faith.

Faith is the victory that moves us from defeated to victorious, from broken to restored, from weary to standing strong.

Counseling Insight: When Defeat Feels Closer Than Victory

Many people in counseling admit they feel overwhelmed by the world. They say things like:

- "I feel like I'm always one step behind."
- "Temptation is stronger than me."
- "I want to overcome, but I keep slipping back."

The truth is, overcoming isn't about your power—it's about who you belong to. If you are born of God, overcoming is already in your spiritual DNA. Faith unlocks what God has already placed within you.

The Reality of Struggles

Being an overcomer doesn't mean you'll never struggle. It means that no struggle can ultimately define or defeat you.

- Joseph was betrayed and imprisoned, but his faith made him an overcomer who rose to lead Egypt.
- David faced giants, sin, and enemies, but he returned to God in faith and overcame.
- Jesus Himself declared: "Be of good cheer; I have overcome the world" (John 16:33).

If Christ overcame, and you are in Him, then overcoming is part of your destiny.

Story: Carla's Breakthrough

Carla came to counseling after years of financial struggles. She said: "Every time I make progress, something knocks me back. I feel defeated before I even try."

Together, we studied 1 John 5:4. Carla began to see her identity differently—not as someone struggling to overcome, but as someone born of God who already carried victory within.

Months later, she testified: "My circumstances didn't change overnight, but my mindset did. I no longer live in defeat—I live as an overcomer."

Practical Counseling Applications

1. **Overcomer Affirmation**
   Say daily: "I am born of God; I overcome the world by faith."
2. **Faith Fuel**
   Identify one area where you feel defeated. Write a Scripture promise over it. Let that promise fuel your faith.
3. **Overcomer Journal**
   Record every small victory (over a bad habit, a negative thought, a fear). Small wins build momentum toward larger breakthroughs.
4. **Shift the Identity**
   When you're tempted to say, "I can't win," replace it with, "I am an overcomer in Christ."

Reflection Questions

- What area of your life feels hardest to overcome right now?
- How does remembering you are "born of God" shift your perspective?
- What practical step of faith can you take today to live as an overcomer?

Prayer

"Lord, thank You that I am born of You and that makes me an overcomer. Strengthen my faith so I no longer live in defeat. Teach me to see myself as You see me—victorious, strong, and full of overcoming power. I trust You to carry me through every battle until I walk fully in the victory You've promised. Amen."

24

Overcometh: The Action of Victory

The Ongoing Battle

To say you are an overcomer (identity) is one thing. To live out the process of overcoming (action) is another. The word nikaō emphasizes movement—conquering, prevailing, pressing forward, and claiming victory again and again.

Being born of God makes you an overcomer. But daily faith in action means you overcometh.

Counseling Insight: Overcoming is Ongoing

Many believers struggle because they expect one victory to settle everything forever. In counseling sessions, I often hear:

- "I thought I overcame fear, but it came back."
- "Didn't I already win this battle? Why am I fighting again?"

The truth is, overcoming is continuous. Just like battles in life keep arising, the action of overcoming keeps recurring. The key is not perfection but persistence. Overcometh means we keep conquering, keep rising, keep prevailing—until the final victory.

Biblical Example

- David didn't just defeat Goliath once; he kept overcoming enemies throughout his life.
- Paul wrote, "We are troubled on every side, yet not distressed... cast down, but not destroyed" (2 Cor. 4:8–9). His life was a continual rhythm of "overcometh."
- Jesus overcame temptation, opposition, the cross—and now empowers us to keep overcoming until the end.

Story: A Cycle of Overcoming

Jason battled with cycles of depression. He would experience victory for a season but then relapse into darkness. He said: "I feel like I failed God because I have to fight this again."

We studied nikaō together. Jason realized that overcoming wasn't a one-time medal—it was an ongoing fight. Every time he chose faith instead of despair, he was overcoming again. His story shifted from shame to perseverance.

The Reward of Overcometh

In Revelation, Jesus makes promises to him that overcometh:

- "To him that overcometh will I give to eat of the tree of life" (Rev. 2:7).
- "He that overcometh shall not be hurt of the second death" (Rev. 2:11).
- "To him that overcometh will I grant to sit with me in my throne" (Rev. 3:21).

Overcoming isn't just for survival now—it's preparation for eternal reward.

Practical Counseling Applications

1. Daily Conquering Prayer
   Each morning pray: "Lord, I overcome today by Your power. Whatever I face, I will prevail."
2. Victory Lens
   See every challenge not as a setback but as another chance to "overcometh."
3. Persistence Practice
   Keep record of times you refused to quit, even if you stumbled. Persistence itself is part of overcoming.
4. Scripture Anchor
   Memorize Revelation 12:11: "And they overcame him by the blood of the Lamb, and by the word of their testimony."

Reflection Questions

- What battle keeps reappearing in your life?
- How can you reframe repeated struggles as opportunities to "overcometh"?
- What eternal reward motivates you to keep fighting?

Prayer

"Lord, I thank You that in Christ, I do not just call myself an overcomer—I live it out daily as I overcometh the challenges before me. Strengthen me to persist when battles return. Teach me that each victory, large or small, is proof that You are with me. And remind me that one day, my overcoming will be complete in Your eternal presence. Amen."

25

This Is the Victory: Conquering the Difficult

Victory Defined

When the Bible speaks of victory, it uses the word nikē, meaning conquest—the success that comes from mastering something difficult. Victory isn't the absence of battles. It's the outcome of battles faced, endured, and overcome.

This truth reshapes how we see hardship. Instead of viewing challenges as signs of failure, we begin to see them as the very soil where victory is grown.

Counseling Insight: Struggle as the Pathway

In counseling, many people express weariness:

- "Why do I have to fight so hard?"
- "Shouldn't victory mean everything gets easier?"
- "I thought God's blessing meant peace, not constant battles."

But Scripture reminds us that victory does not come without conquest. To "master something difficult" means there was a difficulty to face in the first place.

Victory is not the absence of difficulty—it is the proof that you conquered it.

Biblical Examples of Nikē

- Joshua and Israel had to march around Jericho before the walls fell. Their victory came after persistence in obedience.
- Daniel had to face the lions' den, but his conquest came through faithfulness under pressure.
- Jesus faced the cross, and His resurrection was the ultimate nikē—success in mastering the most difficult trial of all.

Story: Overcoming in the Workplace

Renee was struggling at her job, facing constant criticism from her boss. She said: "I feel like I'm failing every day. I just want to quit."

Through counseling, Renee reframed her perspective. Instead of quitting, she prayed daily for strength, asking God to help her "master the difficulty." Over time, she not only endured but excelled, eventually receiving a promotion.

She later said: "Victory wasn't God removing my boss—it was God helping me master the situation."

The Layers of Victory

1. Conquest Over Self – Overcoming fear, doubt, or pride.
2. Conquest Over Circumstances – Learning to thrive in challenges, not just survive them.
3. Conquest Over the Enemy – Resisting the attacks of Satan and standing firm in Christ's authority.

Victory is multi-layered, but it always carries the same core: God's power manifested in your persistence.

Practical Counseling Applications

1. **Victory Journal**
   Write down current difficulties and next to each write: "This will become my conquest."
2. **Reframe Difficulty**
   Instead of saying, "Why me?" begin asking, "What victory is God preparing me for through this?"
3. **Daily Declaration**
   Say: "This is the victory that overcomes the world, even my faith" (1 John 5:4).
4. **Celebrate Small Conquests**
   Every step forward, no matter how small, is a victory in mastering something difficult.

Reflection Questions

- What difficulty are you facing right now that feels like defeat?
- How would your outlook change if you saw it as the soil for victory?
- What small conquest can you celebrate today as part of the bigger victory?

Prayer

"Lord, thank You that victory is not about avoiding challenges but mastering them through Your strength. Help me see my struggles as opportunities for conquest. Remind me daily that faith is the victory that overcomes the world. I trust You to turn every difficulty into proof of Your power. Amen."

26

Next Move: Pressing Beyond What Was

The Call to Keep Moving

Paul's words remind us that the Christian walk is not about staying stuck in yesterday's failures or even yesterday's victories. The phrase "forgetting those things which are behind" does not mean erasing memory, but choosing not to be controlled by the past.

The next move in your life requires releasing yesterday so that you can reach for tomorrow.

Counseling Insight: The Weight of Yesterday

In sessions, many people wrestle with one of two weights:

1. The weight of regret – replaying mistakes, wishing they could undo what's already been done.
2. The weight of nostalgia – clinging to past seasons of success, unable to see that God has more ahead.

Both weights can keep us stuck. But Paul shows us the way forward: release and reach.

Release: Forgetting What's Behind

- Failures – Your mistakes don't define you; God's mercy does.
- Hurts – Past wounds can paralyze, but forgiveness unlocks freedom.
- Achievements – Yesterday's success was good, but it cannot sustain tomorrow's calling.

Reach: Stretching Toward What's Ahead

The word "reaching" suggests an athlete leaning forward in a race. Victory requires leaning into what God is setting before you. This means:

- Expecting new opportunities.
- Embracing fresh assignments.
- Believing that the best chapters of your story have not yet been written.

Story: Moving After Loss

Michael lost his business in a downturn. He came to counseling saying: "I feel like my best days are behind me."

Through prayer and guided reflection on Philippians 3:13, Michael began to see that his loss wasn't the end. He started a small mentoring group for younger entrepreneurs, which not only restored his joy but opened a door for a new career.

Michael's "next move" was hidden inside his loss.

Practical Counseling Applications

1. **Write Down What Needs Releasing**
   Make a list of regrets, hurts, or past glories. Pray over them, and ask God for the grace to release.

2. **Define Your Next Move**

What is God stirring in your heart now? Write it as a declaration: "I am reaching for..."

3. **Create Forward Habits**

Build daily practices—reading, prayer, serving—that point forward, not backward.

Reflection Questions

- What past pain or success is hardest for you to release?
- What new thing do you sense God calling you to reach for?
- How will you discipline yourself to lean forward like an athlete in a race?

Prayer

"Father, I release yesterday into Your hands—my failures, my hurts, and even my victories. I refuse to be bound by what was. Strengthen me to press forward and embrace what You have placed before me. Guide my next move, Lord, so that it glorifies You and leads me into destiny. Amen."

Part VII – More Than a Conqueror

27

Possess What You Know!!

Knowledge Alone Isn't Enough

Many believers live with abundant knowledge of God's Word but fail to walk in it. They can quote promises, recite scriptures, and even encourage others, yet struggle to apply those truths to their own lives.

The Apostle Paul reminds us that it's not enough to hear or know the truth — we must apprehend it. The Greek word katalambanō paints a picture of grabbing hold eagerly and not letting go.

From Knowing to Owning

There is a vast difference between:

- Knowing healing is available and walking in the confidence of being healed.
- Quoting "God provides" and actually trusting Him in financial lack.
- Hearing "God is with me" and boldly facing a storm without fear.

To possess what you know means to convert information into transformation.

Story: The Forgotten Key

Angela kept a key to her storage unit on her key ring but forgot it was there. For years, she paid for the unit without opening it. Inside were family heirlooms, valuable antiques, and even documents that could have saved her money and time.

One day, a friend noticed the key and asked what it was for. Angela finally used it — and realized she had been paying for what was already hers but never accessed.

The promises of God are like that key. If you don't seize them, you'll live as if they don't exist, even while carrying them with you.

Counseling Insight: Why We Hesitate

Many don't apprehend what they know because of:

1. Fear of disappointment – "What if I believe and it doesn't work?"
2. Comfort in familiarity – "I'll stay where I am, even if it's not God's best."
3. Doubt in worthiness – "God does it for others, but not for me."

But Paul urges us to take eagerly — not timidly. God's promises are not fragile glass; they are solid rock.

Practical Steps to Possess What You Know

1. Declare it Out Loud – Faith grows by hearing (Romans 10:17). Speak the promises daily.
2. Act on It – If you believe God will provide, take the step He's leading you to.
3. Refuse to Relinquish – Don't let setbacks cause you to drop what God already placed in your hand.

Reflection Questions

- What promise of God do you know but haven't truly possessed?
- Where have you allowed fear or doubt to keep you from seizing what's yours?
- What practical step can you take this week to apprehend what God has said?

Prayer

"Lord, I refuse to only know Your Word in theory. I choose to seize, to apprehend, and to live out every promise You've spoken. Strengthen my hands to hold on tightly and eagerly to Your truth until it manifests in my life. Amen."

28

Keep Pressing!!!

The Call to Relentless Pursuit

Paul's words in Philippians 3:14 are both inspiring and challenging: "I press toward the mark for the prize of the high calling of God in Christ Jesus."

Notice his language: press. He doesn't say "I stroll" or "I casually walk." Pressing implies resistance, effort, and determination. There will always be forces — discouragement, fear, temptation, delay — that try to hold you back. But the call of God requires forward motion despite opposition.

Pressing Requires Purpose

You won't press toward anything without first identifying the mark. Paul's mark was the prize of fulfilling his high calling in Christ.

What's your mark?

- Living in obedience to God's Word?
- Walking in freedom from old habits?
- Pursuing a God-given dream?
- Leading your family in faith?

When you define your mark, pressing gains direction.

Story: The Marathon Runner

During a marathon, a runner collapsed just half a mile from the finish line. Medical staff rushed to him, but he waved them off, crawled to his knees, and eventually staggered across the line. When asked why he didn't quit, he replied: "My country didn't send me 26 miles to quit at 25 and a half. I came to finish."

That's pressing. It's the mindset that says, "I didn't come this far in faith to give up now."

Counseling Insight: Why Some Stop Pressing

1. Fatigue of the Soul – weariness sets in when results take longer than expected.
2. Distraction – eyes fixed on obstacles instead of the mark.
3. Comparison – watching others finish faster and feeling unworthy.

But pressing isn't about speed — it's about persistence. The race is not to the swift but to those who endure.

How to Keep Pressing

1. Refocus Daily – Remind yourself of your "why."
2. Draw Strength from God – Isaiah 40:31 reminds us that those who wait on the Lord renew their strength.
3. Celebrate Small Wins – Each step forward is victory. Don't wait for the finish line to rejoice.
4. Surround Yourself with Encouragers – Community fuels perseverance.

Reflection Questions

- Where have you been tempted to stop pressing in your walk with God?
- What "mark" are you pressing toward right now?
- What can you do this week to take one more step forward, even if it's small?

Prayer

"Lord, strengthen my heart to press on toward the mark You've set before me. Help me not to look back, not to compare, and not to quit. I fix my eyes on You, the prize of my high calling, and I will keep pressing until I see Your promises fulfilled. Amen."

29

Press

The Nature of Pressing

To press means more than just moving forward — it means to pursue with intensity. Paul's example in Philippians 3:14 shows us that pressing is not optional; it is the posture of every believer who desires to experience the fullness of God's promises.

When you press, you are saying to the world and to the enemy: "I will not be denied. I will not be ignored. I will reach the goal set before me."

Pressing Requires Pursuit

The Greek sense of pressing carries the idea of chasing after something until you apprehend it. Think of a runner chasing the finish line, or a shepherd chasing after a lost sheep until it's found. Pressing doesn't quit because of distance or difficulty — it locks onto the target and won't stop until it's reached.

God calls us to this same relentless pursuit:

- Pursue His presence even when distractions abound.
- Pursue His promises even when delays linger.
- Pursue His calling even when opposition rises.

Not Easily Ignored

The definition reminds us pressing is not easily ignored. That means your persistence will command attention. People may overlook casual faith, but they cannot ignore determined, unwavering faith.

- Bartimaeus, the blind man, pressed by shouting louder when the crowd told him to be quiet.
- The woman with the issue of blood pressed through the crowd until she touched the hem of Jesus' garment.
- Jacob pressed in prayer and wrestled with the angel until he received his blessing.

Pressing faith is not passive; it insists on breakthrough.

Counseling Insight: Why Some Stop Pressing

Many believers give up pressing because:

1. They Mistake Resistance for Rejection – When obstacles rise, they assume God said "no," when in fact He said, "Press."
2. They Grow Weary – The pace drains them because they try pressing in their own strength instead of God's.
3. They Fear Standing Out – Pressing makes you noticeable, and some would rather blend in than risk criticism.

But pressing requires courage. You cannot press quietly into destiny; you must be bold, resilient, and unshakable.

How to Cultivate a Pressing Spirit

1. Anchor Yourself in God's Word – His promises fuel perseverance.

2. Pray with Determination – Pressing prayer is persistent, like the widow before the unjust judge (Luke 18).
3. Push Past Feelings – Pressing is a decision, not a mood.
4. Surround Yourself with Others Who Press – Community keeps momentum alive.

Reflection Questions

• Where have you grown passive instead of pressing in your faith journey?
• What promise of God requires you to press harder right now?
• How can you reframe resistance as confirmation that you're pursuing the right mark?

Prayer

"Lord, give me the strength to press even when I feel weak, to pursue even when I'm resisted, and to persevere until I see Your promises fulfilled. May my faith not be casual, but determined — not easily ignored, but boldly pressing toward the mark You have set for me. Amen."

30

The Power of Pursuit

Pursuit Defines Destiny

Every person who accomplished great things in Scripture did so because they pursued God and His promises. Pursuit is the evidence of desire. You cannot say you want something from God and yet remain still. To pursue means to set your face, your will, and your energy toward what God has placed before you.

David pursued Goliath when others hid. Elijah pursued God's fire when Israel wavered. Paul pursued Christ so fiercely that he counted all other achievements as loss. Pursuit always reveals priority.

Why Pursuit Matters

1. It Aligns Your Focus – Pursuit forces you to ignore distractions and fix your eyes on Jesus.
2. It Proves Your Faith – Faith without pursuit is theory. Faith with pursuit becomes testimony.
3. It Unlocks God's Power – God meets us in movement. As you pursue, heaven responds.

A Pursuit That Cannot Be Ignored

When you exert yourself continuously and vigorously, your faith journey begins to command attention. The world may overlook a casual believer, but it cannot ignore one who pursues Christ relentlessly.

The early church was unstoppable not because of numbers but because of pursuit. Their boldness, persistence, and refusal to quit made them impossible to silence. That same Spirit lives in you.

Counseling Insight: What's Hindering Your Pursuit?

- Fear of Failure – You stop pressing because you fear missing the mark.
- Fatigue of Delay – Waiting too long can tempt you to slow down.
- Frustration with Opposition – The more you press, the more resistance rises.

But pursuit is not measured by ease; it is measured by endurance. You may stumble, but keep moving. You may weep, but keep pressing. You may feel weak, but God's strength is perfected in weakness.

Keys to Keep Pursuing

1. Set Daily Goals in Faith – Pursuit is built one step at a time.
2. Confess God's Word Aloud – Speaking truth keeps the vision alive in your spirit.
3. Stay Accountable – Let others remind you to keep pressing when you feel like giving up.
4. Celebrate Progress – Every step forward is evidence of God's faithfulness.

Reflection Questions

- What dream, promise, or calling has God asked you to pursue with greater intensity?
- How can you renew your energy for pursuit today?
- Who can you invite into your journey to help you keep pressing forward?

Prayer

"Father, ignite within me a spirit of relentless pursuit. Let nothing distract me, discourage me, or defeat me. I will press, I will pursue, and I will not be ignored, because my eyes are fixed on the prize of Christ. Strengthen my steps until I see the fullness of Your promise. Amen."

31

Conqueror: Gain a Decisive Victory

The Final Word: Victory Is Yours

A conqueror does not win by accident. A conqueror doesn't stumble into victory. A conqueror gains a decisive victory—one so clear, so undeniable, that there is no doubt who reigns triumphant.

Romans 8:37 has already declared that you are more than a conqueror through Him that loved you. Now, the Spirit presses the truth deeper: not only do you overcome—you do so with a victory that silences your enemy, strengthens your testimony, and glorifies your God.

What Does a Decisive Victory Look Like?

- When the addiction is broken, not temporarily, but permanently.
- When the chains of fear snap, and courage becomes your new language.
- When sorrow turns into joy, and the very thing that once broke you now builds you.
- When your family line shifts because you refused to quit, and future generations walk free.

A decisive victory is not a half-win. It is not "barely making it." It is God's Kingdom triumph bursting forth in your life so boldly that even the shadows of yesterday cannot deny it.

The Battle Belongs to the Lord

Hear this truth: You do not fight for victory—you fight from victory. At the cross, Jesus declared, "It is finished." The decisive blow against sin, death, and the enemy was already struck. Now, you walk in the manifestation of what Christ has already won.

This means the pressure is not on you to "be enough." Christ is enough. Your role is to believe, to stand, to press, and to hold fast until the victory unfolds in your life.

Counseling Insight: Living as a Conqueror

Some live as survivors, some live as strugglers, but conquerors live with authority. They do not bow to fear, settle for compromise, or retreat when opposition rises. They live with the unshakable conviction that God's Word is true, His promises are sure, and His Spirit is unstoppable.

Ask yourself:

- Where have I been settling for survival instead of conquest?
- What area of my life needs the decisive victory of God today?
- Am I willing to trust Him fully, obey Him boldly, and pursue Him relentlessly until that victory comes?

The Call to Rise

This is the moment. Don't you dare give up. You've pressed, you've pursued, you've endured affliction, you've held fast by faith. Now God calls you to rise as a conqueror.

Lift your head. Straighten your shoulders. Open your mouth and declare with authority:

- I am not defeated.
- I am not forgotten.
- I am not finished.
- I am a conqueror through Christ who loves me.

A Prayer of Decisive Victory

"Father, I thank You that through Christ I am more than a conqueror. Today, I renounce every lie of defeat, every shadow of fear, and every voice of doubt. I declare that Your victory is my portion. I receive it not halfway, not partially, but decisively. Let my life shine as a testimony of Your power, Your faithfulness, and Your unstoppable love. In Jesus' mighty name—Amen."

Final Charge

Reader, this is not the end of your story. This is the beginning of your conquest. Step into tomorrow with the confidence that no weapon formed against you shall prosper. Walk into every battle knowing the outcome is already sealed. Live in abundant faith, because the God who called you, saved you, and filled you with His Spirit is faithful.

You are not just enduring—you are conquering.

You are not just surviving—you are thriving.

You are not just trying—you are triumphing.

Now, go forth. Gain a decisive victory. And never, ever forget: Don't you dare give up!

Dr. Tony Medley Sr. is a pastor, teacher, mentor, and author whose life and ministry have been dedicated to helping people discover the power of God's Word spoken over their lives. Known for his passionate preaching and practical teaching, Dr. Medley has spent decades equipping believers to hear God's voice, walk in their identity in Christ, and live with purpose and bold faith. His ministry extends beyond the pulpit—through books, training materials, stage plays, and discipleship resources—designed to ignite transformation in individuals, churches, and communities.

Dr. Medley combines deep biblical insight with everyday application, ensuring that readers not only understand the Scriptures but also live them out with confidence. With a message that is both prophetic and practical, Dr. Medley inspires people to see themselves through heaven's perspective. He believes every person is "wrapped in the conversation" of God and destined to thrive in His promises.

When he is not writing or teaching, Dr. Medley is serving his church family, mentoring emerging leaders, and enjoying time with his own family, who remain his greatest earthly joy.